STONE TOWER PRESS

Stone Tower Press
7 Ellen Road
Middletown, RI 02842
stonetowerpress.com

Paperback ISBN: 978-1-7345859-2-6

Formatting and cover design by Amy Cole, JPL Design Solutions

The cover image: by makyzz, www.adobestock.com

Printed in the United States of America

For my wife Melissa,
without whom I'd be lost;
&
For Charles Jones, Duncan Bell, Tarak Barkawi,
and Mike Sewell—four wonderful teachers.

CONTENTS

A BRIEF GUIDE TO THE RESEARCH PROCESS

INTRODUCTION

Most research manuals are too long, attempting to be research aid, style guide, and writing coach all in one. In doing so, they become mere reference books; we reach for them only when problems arise. By contrast, this little book aims to explain the seven steps of the research process in a usably concise manner—it can be read in one sitting. Because each step builds upon its predecessor, new researchers should begin by developing an eagle's-eye view of the entire process, something this book seeks to help the reader attain. Without seeing what lies ahead, how is a researcher supposed to know how much time and effort to spend on the step they're currently on? Drivers with a map of the entire route will fare better with the upcoming blind turn or any detour they might encounter along the way.

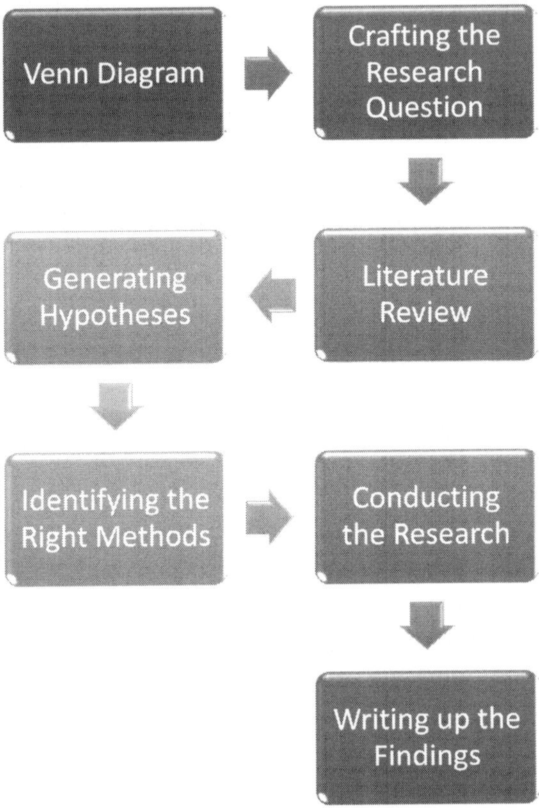
Venn Diagram
Crafting the Research Question
Literature Review
Generating Hypotheses
Identifying the Right Methods
Conducting the Research
Writing up the Findings

The research process isn't intuitive. Rather, it must be taught through the passing of transferrable skills from one person to another and perfected through a researcher's own experience of trial and error. This book speaks of "the" research process, but there really isn't one single process that adequately characterizes the nuances of every research project. This is analogous to when children are taught about "the scientific method," despite the fact that there really is no such thing. Scientists use many methods; these methods change over time; and scientists even disagree about which methods are the right ones.[1] Nevertheless, there are *general* steps that *usually* occur in *most* research projects; and this is enough to allow for textbooks to discuss general steps of scientific research.

This book will be helpful to students at every level—undergraduate, graduate, professional—and applies to all academic subjects: the humanities, engineering, the social sciences, and hard sciences. It contains the absolutely indispensable features of the research process, but no more. If one is doing successful research, one is likely to be following these steps—whether one realizes it or not. This process is therefore essential and unavoidable, which is an excellent reason to want to do it well!

1 For classic works making this point see (Feyerabend 2010) and (Kuhn 1996).

STEP 1:

THE VENN DIAGRAM STAGE

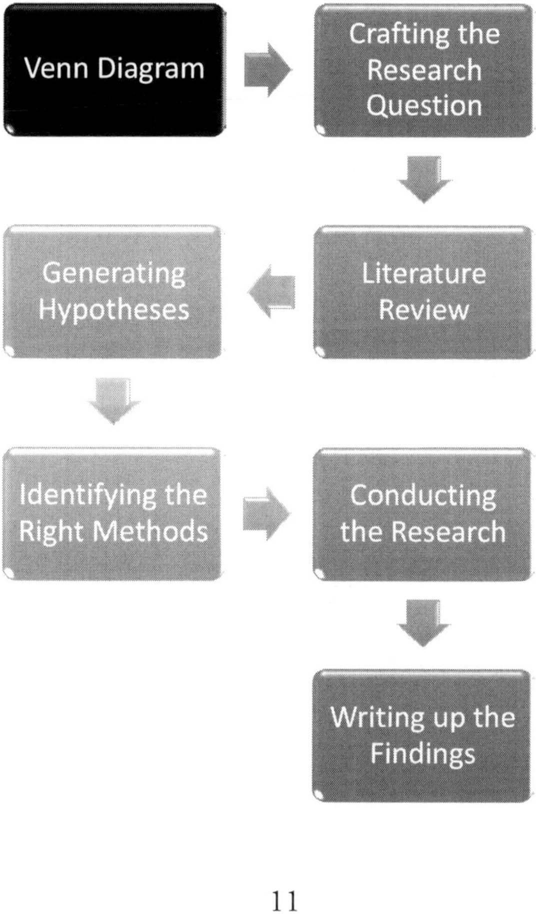

All research begins with overlapping conceptual or topical categories. When a student is asked what their research project is about they typically respond by providing two or three categories between which their topic is situated. For example, an undergraduate student might respond by saying, "I'm doing a senior research project about how culture impacts cyber operations." A master's degree student may respond by stating that their thesis "is on the history of monetary policy during the gold standard era." Or a Ph.D. student may respond by saying "my dissertation examines the concept of truth in formal languages, such as mathematics and logic." Such students often *think* they have a developed research topic but in fact they are merely at what might be called the Venn diagram step. John Venn (1834-1923) was an English logician whose circular diagrams are used to show interconnected relationships between classes or categories. Students should

A research Venn diagram

be perfectly happy to be at this step so long as they realize that is just the beginning. **Real research work begins only after a research question has been carefully crafted**, and such a question has not yet been developed at the Venn diagram step of the research process.

Take a look at our hypothetical undergraduate student's research statement again from above. This young researcher is really saying, whether she recognizes it or not, that her yet-to-be-written research question will have "culture" and "cyber operations" as two of its topic areas. She may have more in mind, but so far she has only articulated these two categories. In fact, by putting them together in one statement, she's revealing that her research question will rest at the intersection—the center of the Venn diagram—between these two categories. But how many questions can one ask within such an intersection? An enormous number! For example, there are lots of different kinds of cultures and activities that could be called cyber operations. These can be combined and recombined in a truly infinite number of possible ways.

The key mistake that nearly every inexperienced researcher makes is to attempt to begin research at this step, when all they have is a pair of overlapping conceptual categories. If a student goes to the library or search engine with a potentially infinite number of possible research questions then almost *everything* they encounter will seem relevant. Researchers will begin filing away book after book, article after article that they errantly think they must become familiar with and categorize in some way in order to proceed. Unsurprisingly, such researchers quickly overwhelm themselves. In the face of mountains of existing information, they quickly become disenchanted, leading to procrastination and eventually underperformance or failure.

The Venn diagram step is important as an intellectual starting point. It gives researchers the opportunity to throw ideas around, brainstorm, and broadly state what concepts, topics, and categories one wants to work with in their project. Statements such as, "I've always been interested in human culture and in cyber operations and wonder if these are related to each other in some way," or, "I want to investigate monetary policy, especially during the period when the gold standard was still in effect," are indicators that one is at the Venn diagram step of the research process. It's a wonderful place to be! Creativity, spontaneity, and a carefree sense of using one's imagination characterize this step. Venn circles come and go during the process of revision at this stage of research—and that fluidity is perfectly normal.

The early steps in the research process are best done in a tactile manner, publicly—in the company of supportive friends or colleagues. For example, a researcher might use a chalkboard, marker board, or simply a sheet of paper, to physically draw out their provisional Venn circles and ask others to scrutinize it with them aloud. A helpful "Are you just interested in gold or in any metal-based monetary system?" might cause one to reconsider their original Venn diagram.

Once one is reasonably sure they have identified the conceptual categories they will use in their research, they are ready to move on to the next step: transforming their Venn diagram into a well constructed research question.

STEP 2:

CRAFTING A RESEARCH QUESTION

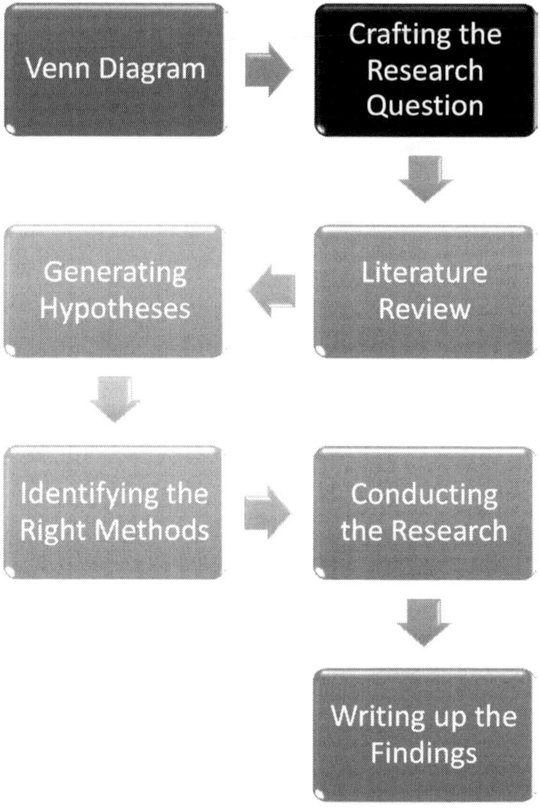

After one has settled on the topical categories of interest and has developed a clear Venn diagram one is ready to begin the next research step—crafting a research question. By that, what is meant is a full and complete question that must begin with a capital letter and end with a question-mark. The question utilizes the conceptual categories found in one's Venn diagram but formulates these into a complete sentence. Let's give this a shot:

Attempt 1: How does culture impact cyber operations?

Notice here that it is written as a real question, not a statement or a fragment. It also includes the hypothetical student's Venn categories. So at least it has the right form, and if one finds that they have written something other than a full question they must rewrite it until it possesses these features. But how does one know if this is a good research question? There is actually a step-by-step process that helps.[2]

2 My articulation of this step in the research process is indebted to the faculty of the Politics and International Studies department at Cambridge University, where I attended graduate school. It was at Cambridge that the iterative stages of crafting a research question was first made explicit to me. Any mistakes in my characterization of this step here are mine alone.

First, write down the research question on a piece of paper, marker board, or chalkboard. Next, draw a box around every key term in the question, letting only completely insignificant terms (e.g. "the," "a," "and") get a pass. Sometimes such terms really are significant and may change the meaning of the question considerably. And sometimes terms can be combined if they naturally go together to form a single concept.

How	does	culture	impact	cyber operations?

Now one must look at the question and ask three things: (i) what facts does the question *assume* to be true, (ii) what specifically does one *mean* by each boxed term, and (iii) is each term *necessary*? Let's start with the analysis of assumptions. Every question assumes that certain things are true which may or may not be. This is so for a very good reason. In order to give meaning to the very terms that appear within the question, certain things must be true, and it is these things that, if untrue, cause major problems later in the research process. If, for example, one's question asks whether computer hardware vulnerabilities, as a class, are a greater problem than software vulnerabilities, the question assumes that both hardware and software vulnerabilities exist. It also assumes that hardware and software vulnerabilities are separable in some meaningful way to allow for comparisons. Since some hardware vulnerabilities can be mitigated through software updates, perhaps this is even an unjustified assumption for one's purpose. At the very least one must be aware of the assumptions they are making when doing research. These assumptions must be acknowledged and made explicit in the writing of the research paper.

The question in *Attempt 1* above rests upon one major assumption, that culture does in fact impact cyber operations, otherwise it would be formulated simply as "Does culture impact cyber operations?" If a researcher decides they'd like to revise their question at this step, removing this assumption by dropping the "How," such a revision is perfectly fine. In doing so, one has both identified a key assumption and a term that was unnecessary to the researcher's revised goal. If, rather, the researcher seeks to accept this assumption, they can do so as well—making note of it for future acknowledgement in the final paper. For our purposes here, supposed the researcher decided to revise their question (Attempt 2) in light of this assumption.

Attempt 2: Does culture impact cyber operations?

Now each term in the question must be analyzed (i.e. their meaning must be further refined). The three terms that standout as in need of semantic fine-tuning are "culture," "impact," and "cyber operations." In almost every case, the terms used in initial research questions are far too broad. Researchers typically leave the context that provides significance to their words implicit, so the task of refinement involves making these contextual features explicit by adding more words to the question—often modifiers, such as adjectives—or substituting more specific words for terms that were at first too general. For example, suppose our hypothetical research student was actually thinking about examples such as Russia's cyber operation against the US Presidential Election in 2016, or the state-sponsored *Stuxnet* attack on Iran's nuclear enrichment facility at Natanz. In other words, it was the national security culture of state actors that the researcher implicitly meant by "culture" and it was offensive cyber-attacks specifically that they had in mind. Finally, what about the term "impact"? An impact occurs when an object hits another object. That's its literal meaning. In this case, the use is metaphorical and one should always try to avoid the use of metaphor within a research question to avoid ambiguity. Suppose our researcher, upon reflection, states that what was meant by "impact" was a relationship between cause and effect—that is, a *causal* relationship. Taking this into account, the question can be revised as follows.

Attempt 3: Does a nation's security culture affect its offensive cyber operations?

Now we're really starting to get somewhere because the question's key terms are becoming refined enough that actual research can begin to be performed. Sometimes the meaning of an important term can be established by reference to existing research, whether already known to the researcher or discovered through a query of an academic database. In the case of "security culture," for example, suppose the researcher already knows that a number of authors have discussed this concept in a way that is helpful for this research.[3] In that case, the term "security culture" can be left in the research question because an operative meaning has been found and will be explicitly articulated within

3 For example, both K.C. Gustafson (2010) and Stephen Welch (2013) have written extensively on the concept of security cultures within the context of international relations and security studies.

the paper. In fact, by leaning on previous research to bind one's terms, the beginnings of a reference list or bibliography has been established. Continuing on, since a nation's "offensive cyber operations" encompass a huge number of things, this too needs further refinement. Does this mean, for example, the manner in which such operations are ordered (e.g. the chain of command), the resources allocated (e.g. as a proportion of GDP), or the types of operations utilized (e.g. denial of service, phishing)? Choosing the last of these, the question can be further revised.

Attempt 4: Does a nation's security culture affect the types of offensive cyber operations it employs?

Perhaps at this point it seems clear that in order to answer this question one would need to look at every nation, or at least a sufficient sample of nations, and this is something the researcher does not think they have the time or resources to do. A simple way to solve this would be to focus on a smaller subset of nations—perhaps even just one. The nation of choice may be determined by interest, but equally by mundane factors such as one's access to research material.

Attempt 5: Does Russia's security culture affect the types of offensive cyber operations it employs?

At last! This is a properly scoped question for a research project. Further refinements can always be made, of course. If one were an historian one might vary the question slightly by specifying a time-period (e.g. "Did Russia's security culture affect the types of offensive cyber operations it employed from 2005-2016?"). But this question is clearly refined, and the researcher is far better prepared to begin research having crafted a well-developed research question than they were at the Venn diagram step.

The refinement of an adequate research question **may take weeks of hard work**. That investment pays huge dividends as the research process moves forward! This should not be seen as a static process. Later findings may cause a researcher to go back and further enhance or adjust their question still more. It is also beneficial to share one's attempted research questions with others, particularly with experienced researchers and subject matter experts. Outsiders often see meanings, assumptions, and aspects of preliminary research questions that remain stubbornly out of view from the researcher crafting the question.

STEP 3:

THE LITERATURE REVIEW

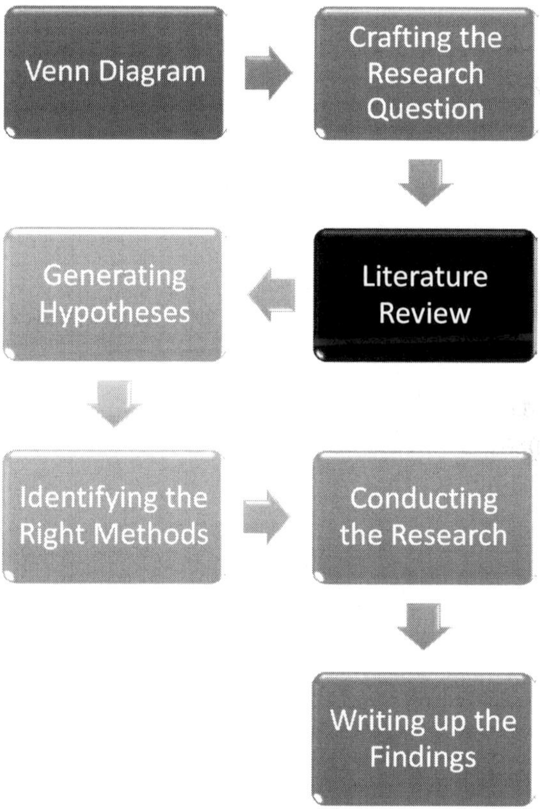

Now that an adequate research question has been crafted, researchers must find out if anyone has already answered it before. To do this one does something called a "literature review." The word "literature" here doesn't have to do with Shakespearian plays or the *The Adventures of Tom Sawyer.* Rather, it signifies the written works relating to a certain topic or subject. The literature on English poetry will be vast, while the literature on household plumbing that references pipes of a certain diameter will be quite small. **A literature review is an analysis of what has been published on topics closely related to one's research question.** It involves searching libraries, search engines, and online databases for material relevant to answering the research question. As noted above, a library's query tool is a great place to begin (and often end) a literature review, as it provides access to a large sample of books, academic articles, and other resources. The use of Boolean searches [for example: ("security culture") AND (("nation state") OR ("nation-state"))] and other techniques allow one to whittle down a potentially daunting number of sources to a few dozen that are specifically relevant to one's question.

When conducting a literature review it is rarely necessary to read an entire book or academic article to discover whether a source is germane to one's research question. Reading through the abstract, using key word searches, inspecting the bibliography or index, or skimming the article or book chapter, are all time-saving analysis techniques.

Once one discovers a source of interest and relevance, one can create what researchers call an "annotated bibliography." An annotated bibliography includes the bibliographical reference information followed by descriptive and evaluative paragraphs or sentences (i.e. the annotation). The description and evaluation should always be from the perspective of the researcher's own project, and guided, as always, by the research question. It is not a book report. If a researcher finds, once they read the source carefully, that it bears little ultimate relevancy to their research question, one must set it aside. As Tarak Barkawi, Professor of International Relations at the London School of Economics, once told me: "the argument is sovereign!" By this he meant that each sentence of one's final research product or paper—which will be the culmination of a tremendous amount of work, all captured in various annotations, working paragraphs, and other reference materials—must contribute to establishing, justifying, and explaining one's thesis, which is the researcher's answer to their research question. Everything else one discovered, found interesting, wrote paragraphs or pages about, and so on, but which did not ultimately move the researcher's argument forward must, like chips of wood on a carpenter's floor, be set aside.

Annotated Bibliography: An Example Entry

Gustafson, K.C. 2010. "Echo of Empires: Russia's Inheritance of Byzantine Security Culture." *Journal of Slavic Military Studies* 23(4): 574-596.

Gustafson argues that the way the Byzantines managed their security and intelligence was a function of the state's political culture, the same political culture that was later inherited by the Russian state, and which has served the Soviet and subsequent post-Soviet Russian state (Gustafson 2010). This analysis supports the conjecture that a deeply ingrained security culture underlies superficial changes in governmental structure, from the Byzantines to today. If that is so, the tactics utilized by the modern Russian state (e.g. offensive cyber operations) ought to bear the mark of this security culture.

Each entry within an annotated bibliography can consist of as little or as much information and commentary as one deems appropriate for that source. In its entirety, the combined entries of an annotated bibliography should achieve three things:

- **Determine whether the research question has been answered before.** If so, the researcher must decide whether they agree with the answer or not. If they agree, there is no more work to be done and the research question must be changed—even if only slightly—to maintain its originality. If the researcher doesn't agree, their originality rests, partly or solely, on their ability to argue against an established point of view, and the reasons for the disagreement will reveal the path forward. It could be, for example, that the basis of the disagreement lies in a perceived insufficiency of the research methods used in previous studies. Perhaps the sample sizes were inadequate. If so, the researcher's task may be to reproduce existing research with an adequate sample. Or perhaps ambiguities are detected in the meaning of the terms employed in existing research, thereby affecting its clear interpretation and application. In this case, originality is attained by clarifying concepts and showing how this elucidation changes the way the research is applied. These are just a few reasons why a researcher may disagree with existing scholarship.

- **Motivate the reader's interest in the question.** A researcher should never assume that readers immediately understand the significance of their research question. Readers may not have the background knowledge to do so, or they may think the answer is trivial. Good researchers explain to their audience why the research question is important and how their results are new and interesting. This is called motivating the research question and it can be accomplished in a number of ways. Perhaps the question has never been asked or answered. Perhaps it has been asked but the answers researchers have offered were incomplete or assumed something that is actually false. By showing the reader that any of these are the case through one's literature review one has generated interest in the minds of one's readers. A literature review often makes explicit the shortcomings of its predecessors. It says, "Authors A, B, and C, did a study on something similar to my study but failed to take into account such and such," and, "while authors D, E, and F, did take into account such and such, they failed to use an adequate method," therefore, "this study at last employs the correct method and takes such and such into account." By the end of one's literature review, the readers should understand exactly where the present research fits into the existing body of research and why it is new and important.

- **Provide sufficient background to the reader so that they are able to follow one's argument.** Most readers will need a certain amount of information given to them in order that they might understand what the research attempts to show or explain. For example, in the case of our hypothetical research question, a reader cannot be expected to know that contemporary Russia shares with the Byzantine Empire its security culture. The literature review can discuss works, such as the Gustafson example above, that establish that connection, thereby freeing the researcher from the obligation to re-establish that idea and allowing the argument to move forward with that idea's implications for offensive cyber operations.

Once a researcher has a sufficient annotated bibliography one has effectively surveyed the scholarly work predating the researcher's current project. Thus, combining the last two steps, one has asked and refined a new research question and shown why attaining the answer to that question is valuable. And in the annotated bibliography one has generated the reference material necessary to properly inform one's reader about the background information required to make sense of the current research project.

STEP 4:

GENERATING HYPOTHESES

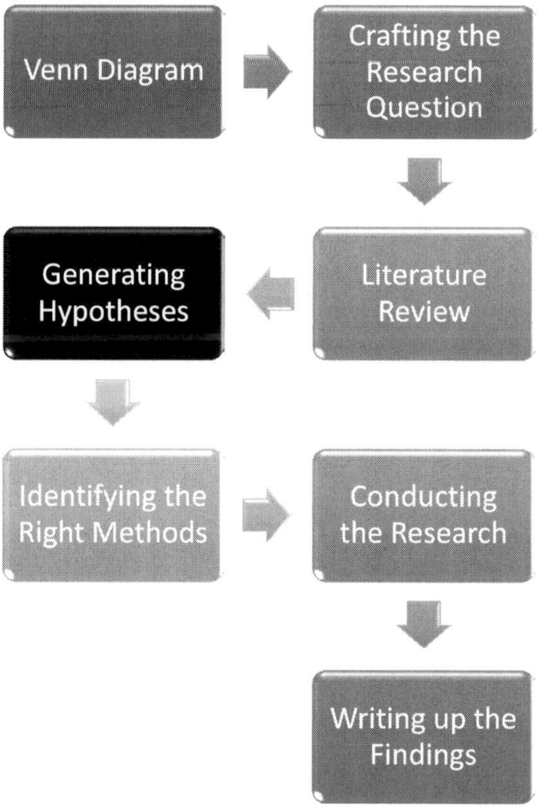

Not all research is empirical in nature. Research may rearrange known facts or concepts in interesting new ways to argue for conclusions that nobody has yet thought of. Albert Einstein's *Special Theory of Relativity* was largely of this kind. Fruitful research conducted on questions involving definitions, theory, history, or ethical and normative topics often fall into this category. However, a great deal of research seeks to answer questions that do require new data and the parsing of new observations. In such cases, researchers should seek to generate hypotheses prior to performing the data collection and analysis.

Hypotheses are specially-crafted guesses or predictions at what the data will reveal. More accurately, an hypothesis is a supposition or proposed explanation made on the basis of limited evidence as a starting point for further more detailed investigation. The suppositions shouldn't come out of thin air but should be justified by the existing literature or be reasonable extrapolations from the research question's meaning. Multiple hypotheses are often generated for a given research question. For example:

Does Russia's security culture affect the types of offensive cyber operations it employs?

H_1 Russia's security culture strongly determines what types of offensive cyber operations it employs.

H_2 Russia's security culture partly determines what types of offensive cyber operations it employs.

H_3 Russia's security culture does not determine what types of offensive cyber operations it employs.

Good hypotheses help researchers by articulating testable answers to the research question asked. In doing so, correct investigative methods are more readily identified. An hypothesis must be specific enough to be testable, and the criterion for its truth or falsity must be made clear *prior* to the research commencing. In the examples above, the phrases "strongly determines," "partly determines," and "does not determine," are terms of ordinary language that need to be directly linked to criteria for their truth or falsity. In science this is sometimes called *operationalizing* terms.[4] While crafting the example research question, the meaning of the term "security culture" was found within the academic literature, and supposing that further research showed Russia's security culture to consist of eight attributes (e.g. the belief that notable state affairs

4 The classic statement on operationalization comes in (Bridgman 1927).

are done in secret; the view that the governmental regime, not the people, is the referent object for security; and so on), then the falsification criterion for H_1 might be operationalized by postulating that if six or more attributes are found to be present in at least 80% of the analyzed cases then this will mean that H_1 has been confirmed. In other words, this is the operational meaning of the term "strongly determines" in H_1. Operationalizing helps bring clarity to key terms and avoid the problem of confirmation bias—the tendency to interpret data in such a way that it confirms what one already believes.

Once again, not all research questions are empirical in nature and may not, therefore, require generating hypotheses. Those that do, however, benefit from the careful articulation and refinement of testable propositions. Having generated hypotheses, researchers are ready for the next step: identifying the right methods to use to test the hypotheses or otherwise answer the research question.

STEP 5:

IDENTIFYING THE CORRECT METHODS

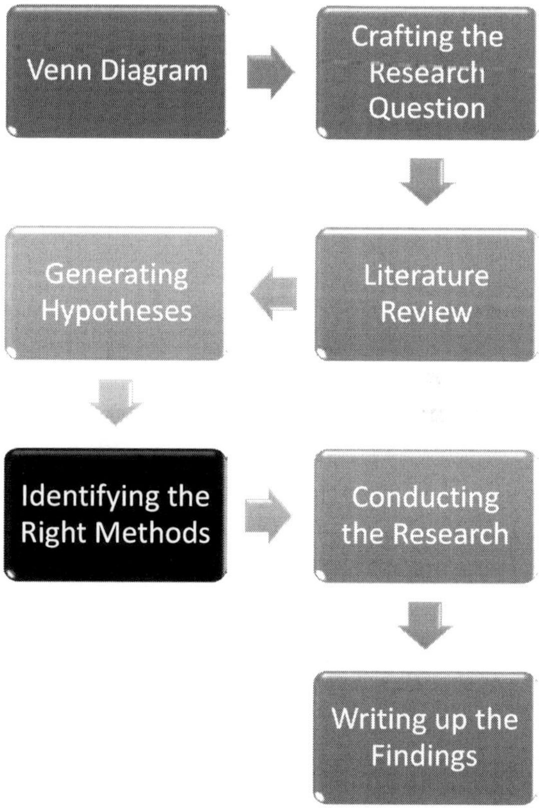

Most researchers, even many published ones, fail to distinguish discussions about "methods" from those of "methodology," and they tend to use the word "methodology" to incorrectly describe the methods they use. But these are different concepts. A method is a specific structured way of performing some research task, while a method · *ology* (from the Greek: λόγος, *logos*, meaning "discursive or rational speech" regarding something) is a philosophical view *about* methods—including their content, employment, and legitimacy.[5]

Many methodological debates center on the nature of knowledge and the human mind's relation to the world. A methodological *positivist*, for example, argues that the mind is sufficiently separate from the world it observes through sensory experience, and by extension the data gathered thereof, that when performed correctly, research methods, be they quantitative or qualitative, lead to neutral objective conclusions. Descriptions of observational data are theory-neutral, for the positivist, and can therefore confirm or falsify empirical hypotheses in a straightforward way. By contrast, a methodological *reflectivist* (or

5 One of the best discussions of the distinction between method and methodology appears in (Jackson 2016, 26-57). Although Jackson's discussion takes place within the context of political science it is applicable elsewhere.

epistemological holist) argues that observation is theory-laden; that is, how we describe what our senses tell us depends to a significant degree upon other beliefs we already hold.[6] Therefore, research methods do not observe neutral data and research conclusions are strongly biased by the interests and beliefs of the researcher. Positivism and reflectivism are only two positions along a spectrum of methodological views.

Most undergraduate research assumes a positivist methodology, particularly in the so-called "hard" sciences, such as physics, chemistry, and the like. This is partly due to the relatively uncontroversial nature of the observation data with which these sciences work, leading to less concern about observational bias. Positivism has also become the assumed methodological position for much of the rest of society, even for those who have never heard the word "methodology." This probably has to do with the exalted cultural position enjoyed by the hard sciences. Researchers working in the humanities and social sciences, by contrast, have been much more open to non-positivist methodological views. This again partly reflects the more

6 For a defense of the philosophical basis of positivism, see (Neurath 1959, 199-208) and (Ayer 1959, 228-243); for one of reflectivist holism see (Quine and Ullian 1978, 20-49) and (Sellars 1956).

indeterminate nature of the observation data that are the concern of anthropology, psychology, economics, political science, cultural studies, history, and the like.

Setting methodology aside, one can split research *methods* into two major groupings—quantitative methods and qualitative methods. Quantitative methods apply to information that can be expressed in numerical categories or relationships (e.g. numbers, comparisons, and statistics). Qualitative methods typically involve the careful in-depth study of a much smaller number of cases. There is a natural research tradeoff between numerical breadth and qualitative depth. A study of the password habits of thousands of computer users allows researchers to make very powerful inferences about the password habits of large populations of computer users. However, simply in order to run such a large study, researchers must necessarily reduce interaction with their research subjects—for example, by using questionnaires that can be disseminated and completed *en masse*. On the other hand, by performing in-depth interviews with a few dozen computer users, each carefully selected as representatives of the population about which one wants to make inferences, researchers may gain deeper insight by gaining access to much more detailed and contextual information about why people make password-related decisions. Ideally, researchers could perform in-depth interviews with thousands of people. But in most cases, the time and resources involved in such an endeavor are prohibitive.

There are many types of *quantitative* analyses. A statistical regression analysis, for example, is a quantitative method used to determine the degree of variation in an output variable (y) that is attributable to one or more input variables (x). Descriptive statistics allow one to calculate numbers that tell researchers about the distribution of a data-set, for example a sample mean, range, and standard deviation. *Z*-tests and *t*-tests are statistical comparisons that allow one to determine, for example, whether a difference between two sample means is statistically significant, and so on. Quantitative analysis is appropriate when one's research question asks about quantifiable relationships and the researcher has access to a sufficiently robust amount of numerical data to answer the question. There are many excellent data analysis books and websites dedicated to quantitative methods, whether general statistics textbooks or books dedicated to specific types of data analysis (e.g. time-series analysis).[7]

7 For a great short primer in data analysis from an industry point of view, see (Wheeler 2000).

As noted above, *qualitative* analysis generally trades numerical breadth for contextual depth. By focusing on a comparatively smaller number of cases, qualitative analysis allows researchers to uncover a tremendous amount of data that superficial numerical relationships cannot. This adds textured nuance to a researcher's understanding of the phenomena in question. The paradigmatic case study method, for example, uses the careful analysis of a small number of representative cases, of, say, election interferences by Russia, to make general inferences about Russian election interferences—or even about election vulnerabilities broadly. Structured interviews, similarly, allow researchers to understand the motives, beliefs, desires, and intentions that form the basis of human behavior—for example, in the password-related choices example above. Discourse analysis is a qualitative method that studies the use of language relating to a topic of interest. By tracking how language is used, researchers may gain deep insights into what people may think, feel, or believe—and by extension how they behave. There are a number of good resources dedicated to qualitative methods.[8]

Some research questions require both the employment of quantitative and qualitative methods to find a satisfactory

8 See (King *et al.* 1994) for an excellent source on qualitative research.

answer. This is often referred to as "mixed-methods" research. There is no *a priori* reason to exclude one or the other type of method. Rather, the research method chosen should be a natural extension of one's research question.

Once the research method has been identified, one is ready for the next step: conducting the research itself. Sometimes one discovers while conducting research that the chosen methods are inadequate to their research task, or must be altered in some way due to hitherto unimagined constraints. This is perfectly fine, and one simply needs to move back a step and make the necessary adjustments.

STEP 6:

CONDUCTING THE RESEARCH

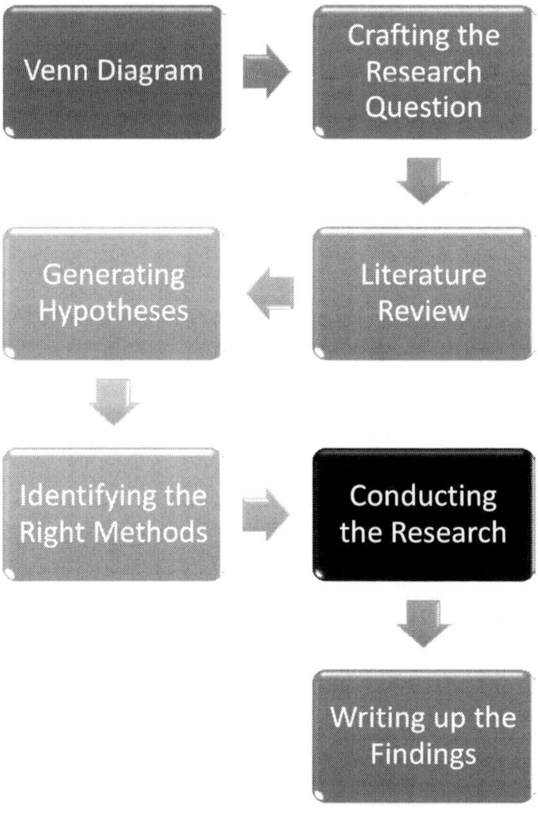

At this step, one performs the data collection and analysis, writes the computer code, gives sufficient thought to ethical, normative, or nonempirical scholarship, and so on. There is less to say about this step of the research process because this is the step of *action*—performing the tasks necessary to generate results.

Research must be conducted in an ethical way. Researchers are expected to exhibit complete integrity in all of their activities. Academic dishonesty, including plagiarism of any type, violates this principle. Plagiarism is the act of presenting another's words, ideas, or work as one's own, whether accidentally or deliberately. Another issue that sometimes arises is the artificial generation of data-sets or results. This too is never justified and is one of the central reasons behind the scientific norm that one must be ready to make one's data available to other researchers so that the study can be independently reproduced.

Research involving human subjects must be approved by an Institutional Review Board (IRB). Even seemingly innocuous research tasks, such as asking people's permission to participate in a survey, must receive IRB approval before commencing. The IRB review and approval process can be quite lengthy, so adequate time must be allocated.

STEP 7:

WRITING UP THE FINDINGS

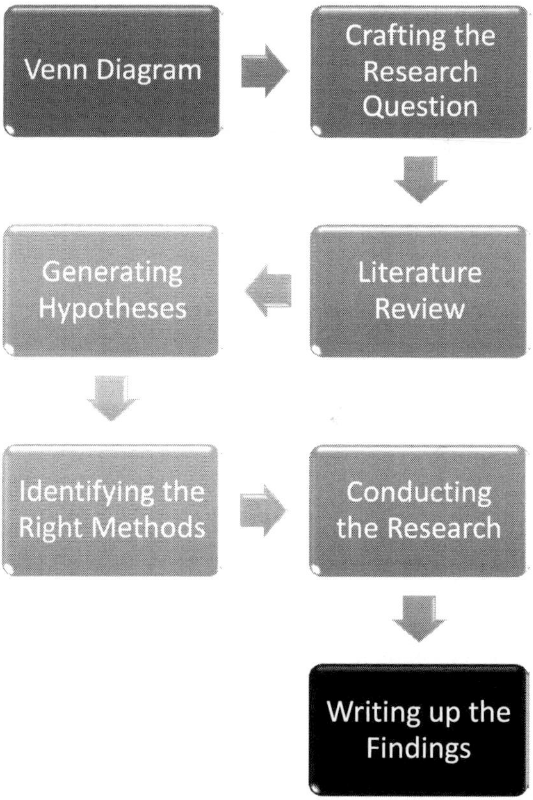

At this point, one has moved from the Venn diagram step, through the generation of the research question, the literature review, and hypothesis generation. The correct methods were identified to answer the research question and the subsequent data gathering and analysis has been undertaken. But all of this is ultimately meaningless if the results aren't shared with others in a way that is clear and understandable. The research process culminates in a research product that conveys not just the results but also a good amount of information from the previous six steps. Typically this takes the form of a research paper, book (if the project is lengthy), book chapter, or presentation.

Many students receive scholarly information strictly from textbooks or academic lectures, which nicely summarize peer-reviewed scholarly research and make it intelligible to the student audience. However, this means that students are sometimes less directly familiar with the sort of academic writing they are then asked to produce for their own senior thesis, master's thesis or doctoral dissertation. It will therefore be useful to describe what makes academic writing unique and how one might improve one's own conveyance of their research conclusions.

What is academic writing?

Academic writing differs from other writing in its epistemic role, its manner of expression, and its standards for publication. Let's take these one by one. The term "epistemic" comes from the Greek word ἐπιστήμη (pron. epistēmē) which means "knowledge" or "understanding." Academic writing is ultimately meant to **persuade an audience of some conclusion by means of valid logical inference** rather than mere rhetoric, sophistry, or appeals to tradition or authority. This is called making an "argument" and the conclusion is called a "thesis." The term "argument" here isn't the same as when someone says they've had an argument with their sibling or spouse. Rather, in academia, an argument is a line of reasoning from premises or established facts to a conclusion or thesis.

This knowledge-building role means that academics must express themselves differently than novelists, speech writers, entertainers, and so on. Academics must back up any claim they make by referencing the primary study or observation that first established the referenced facts, or by citing secondary sources that reported on these primary sources. So academic writing uses **sourcing, citation, and bibliography** to keep track of the origins of every claim made. When conjectures are put forward they are identified explicitly as such. The activity of citing sources must be undertaken carefully and in accordance with the established citation system for the domain of inquiry under consideration. For example, while this book utilizes the author-date system, which is often used in the sciences and social sciences, other systems, such as the notes-system, are more common in the humanities.

Academic writing is also often full of **words that may be unfamiliar** to student audiences. Why? Because students are usually relative beginners and most academic writing has as its intended audience older more experienced scholars. When anyone encounters an unfamiliar word they must either attempt to gain an understanding of what the unfamiliar word means from its context or look it up in a dictionary.[9] This is true whether one is reading a newspaper, Tolstoy's *Anna Karenina*, or a motorway billboard. Reading should be an *activity* (notice the root of this word – active) not a passive enterprise. Language isn't merely a container or vehicle within which ideas are placed for the purpose of communication. Rather,

9 For a wonderful essay justifying the use of words that might be unfamiliar to an author's audience, see (Buckley 1986).

language *constitutes* these ideas, and the more words one becomes familiar with the more one experiences.

Academic writing also differs from other forms in the standards required for its publication. Academic journals and books undergo a process of **blinded peer review**. That is, the author's name and institutional affiliation are typically removed from the submitted manuscript and then sent to multiple experts within the field, whose identities are also withheld from the author, for a blind review. Most manuscripts receive meticulous criticism and are either rejected or are sent back to the author with a request to resubmit the manuscript after dealing with any deficiencies found by the reviewers. Nonacademic writing, such as newspaper and magazine articles, blog posts, website content, and so on, usually need only satisfy the editors, who usually know the author's identity—potentially allowing all sorts of bias into the process. This isn't to say that blinded peer-review is perfect, but the process of publishing in academia is more rigorous than elsewhere. In academic writing, nonacademic sources should *supplement* but not replace proper academic sourcing. Nonacademic sources can helpfully facilitate discussion or make vivid to an audience conclusions established by rigorous academic work.

Furthermore, academic writing usually must **break new ground**, however incremental, to be published; and this is often achieved, particularly in the sciences, by leveraging the expertise of multiple authors. Novelty typically takes two forms. First, an academic may perform a new study that others haven't yet performed, thereby introducing the world to a new set of facts. Second, an academic may rearrange old facts in a new way, thereby showing the world that new inferences are possible. Sometimes, of course, both of these are accomplished within the same piece of academic writing.

One final point to make about academic writing is that unlike other forms of expression, such as e-mails, texts, and in everyday conversation, the **use of the first-person**—the "I/we" perspective—in academic writing is kept to a minimum. In high school this is often taught in an overly strident or draconian manner, as if the word "I" never appears in scholarly work. This is simply false; it does so appear. However, since the purpose of academic writing is to persuade others through scientific inference, the third-person—the "he/she/it/they" perspective—is the most appropriate point of view overall to adopt. Yet if a situation arises where the first-person is needed, it is best to simply use it rather than create a tortured sentence just to avoid its use. The rule is: if you mean "I," say "I," but you shouldn't mean "I" very often in academic writing.

Improving one's academic writing

Have you ever heard someone describe themselves as "not a math person"? Research has shown that to be a myth. Unless the topic is higher-end mathematics (e.g. quantum physics), nearly everyone can be great at math so long as they practice and put in the work. The same is true of writing. **Good writing is difficult and takes practice**, but nobody should describe themselves as "a bad writer" unless they simply mean that they haven't put in the time, effort, and practice to become a good writer. This is as true of academic essays as it is of poetry and fiction.[10]

Great writers are great readers. **To write well one must read well**. Reading well begins by selecting great texts from which one absorbs—sometimes without realizing it—correct grammar usage, new vocabulary, effective

10 Edgar Allan Poe (1846) wrote a wonderful essay that I would strongly recommend entitled "The Philosophy of Composition," which describes the detailed and methodical process required to write his most famous poem, "The Raven." In it, he dispels the myth that literary creativity has a non-rational basis and must therefore result from inexplicable causes.

sentence construction, appropriate paragraphing, and a host of other skills. If one seeks to write excellent essays, one ought to read accomplished general essayists such as Ralph Waldo Emerson, C.S. Lewis, or George Orwell. Those seeking to improve one's writing of essays in a particular subject—philosophy, for example—should read skillful essayists in that subject, such as Richard Rorty, James Rachels, or Michael Walzer.[11]

Reading well also requires time, enough to fully absorb an essay's content without distraction. This means actively planning to read when one is at one's best—unhurried, alert, and able to immerse oneself. An essay doesn't have to be read in one sitting, and great essays should be read multiple times. Some writing is so profound, so full of insight and ideas, that one cannot really read them for the first time, so to speak, until one has already read it once or twice before. Plato's *Republic* is writing of this caliber, as is the poetry of Emily Dickinson.

11 Recommended essays from these authors include "Character" by Ralph Waldo Emerson (2000, 528-535), "The Inner Ring" by C.S. Lewis (2001, 141-157), "Politics and the English Language" by George Orwell (1981, 156-170), "Philosophy as a Kind of Writing: an essay on Derrida" by Richard Rorty (1982, 90-109), "The Challenge of Cultural Relativism" by James Rachels (2019, 14-31), and "Political Action: The Problem of Dirty Hands" by Michael Walzer (1973, 160-180).

Reading well is also an active process. The mantra I give to my students is: **you aren't reading unless you're writing**. Students should have a physical notebook next to them as they read so that they can record the author's thesis, main points, and, even more importantly, capture the student's own thoughts, observations, and potential objections.[12] Very few people can read through academic writing and remember the argument's details weeks or months later without having them written down. By including both information about the text and one's own observations, thoughts, and criticisms, the notebook keeps a record not just of the text but of *one's reading of the text*. Adding the bibliographical information at the top and referencing page numbers along the side next to each thought or main point gives the reader a handy reference tool to use in one's later writing.

Great writers strive for **clarity in their manner of expression**. George Orwell's previously referenced essay "Politics and the English Language," enumerates six rules writers should follow to achieve this:

12 Research continues to show that longhand notes are superior to computer notetaking (Mueller and Oppenheimer 2014).

1. Never use a metaphor, simile, or other figure of speech which you are used to seeing in print.

2. Never use a long word where a short one will do.

3. If it is possible to cut a word out, always cut it out.

4. Never use the passive where you can use the active.

5. Never use a foreign phrase, a scientific word, or a jargon word if you can think of an everyday English equivalent.

6. Break any of these rules sooner than say anything outright barbarous.

Much academic writing runs afoul of Orwell's six rules, but most *great* academic writers follow his advice, even when appearances seem otherwise. For example, the reason William F. Buckley Jr. (in the essay referenced in the footnote above) uses "eristic" [ERISTIC: (i ris/ tik) adj. of or provoking controversy, or given to sophistical argument and specious reasoning] to describe a judge's behavior, is because, Buckley explains, the word captures exactly the meaning he wished to convey. No other word would do. The alternative would have been, for Buckley, to craft a longer descriptive phrase which would violate Orwell's second rule. Of course, Buckley was likely aware that by choosing "eristic" some readers would be forced to look up its meaning in a dictionary. But he accepted this as the price to pay for the semantic precision he needed. Similarly, Orwell's warning against the use of "pretentious diction" (e.g. foreign words, scientific words, or jargon) is based upon his view that such vocabulary is often "used to dress up a simple statement and give an air of scientific impartiality to biased judgements." But note that this is not violated by, for example, one doctor's note to another stating that her patient "has contracted *varicella*" (chicken pox). This is because, due to their common training, both doctors are presumed to have this term as part of their working vocabularies.

The secret to writing well rests in three tasks: (a) choosing the correct audience with which to communicate, (b) using an appropriate real person (preferably someone one knows well) to represent that audience, and (c) always keeping that **representative person** in mind as each sentence is written. The representative individual has been appropriately selected if she possesses the same background information, education level, vocabulary, and set of interests as the audience with whom the writing seeks to communicate. By writing *to her* one will ensure one is effectively choosing the right words, explaining what needs to be explained, and so on. As John R. Trimble (2010), the author of my favorite book on writing, notes, bad writing mostly stems from an author's forgetting that they are trying to communicate to a real audience. Following these three steps helps mitigate this pitfall.

Great academic writing has a **clear structure**. A clear organization helps the reader determine what argument is being made, what evidence is being offered, what portion of the writing simply describes work by previous authors, and what portion offers something new. The importance of structure can be seen in the way academic journal articles are organized into commonly occurring sections or categories. Students should familiarize themselves with these:

- **Abstract**: a short summary of the article, its thesis, and main point appearing at the beginning of the article (often in smaller or italicized font).

- **Introduction**: academics often begin articles by stating their research question, by stating their thesis plainly up front, or motivating the reader to want to continue by showing a gap in the literature that the article promises to fill.

- **Literature review**: academic articles usually review past academic work on the question taken up by the present article, or, if the question hasn't been asked before, the article reviews work closely related to its own question. Sometimes it is within the literature review that the author discusses gaps in the scientific work that the article addresses.

- **Data analysis or research method** (often called "Methodology," errantly, as was explained above): if a new study has been conducted, this section explains how the data was gathered, processed, and analyzed. Sometimes authors attempt to justify their methods as legitimate for the task at hand, the data types used, or the question asked.

    - Sometimes methods are used that may not be familiar to readers. If, for example, a statistical method is unfamiliar to a reader, who is left puzzled by tables of resultant coefficients, they must either research the method themselves or trust the author (and the peer-review system of publication) to have done the analysis correctly and made valid conclusions from the data.

- **Conclusions**: this section combines the literature review (known facts) with the data analysis (new facts) to produce novel claims, to refute older conclusions, or to open up the possibility of original and potentially more fruitful questions.

- **Final summary**: academic writing often ends by summarizing what the article accomplished, walking the reader through each of the aforementioned steps.

In short, a good academic essay states its research question and thesis early (even in the title or first sentence)[13] and telegraphs to the reader the argument's main points which the author will make in order to justify the thesis. It then does what it says; it follows these steps, using academic sourcing to contextualize the author's argument against what others have said. As stressed earlier, non-academic sources, such as websites, news articles, and so on, are used only to *supplement*—not replace—proper

13 I'm particularly fond of essays that begin by asking the research question, as I did (Hatfield 2017) in an article about the ethics of treason, which began with "When is someone morally justified in spying against his or her own country?"

academic sourcing. Toward the end, or throughout, good essays will discuss counterarguments that can be made against the thesis, its main points, or any assumptions employed. Good essays don't necessarily have to provide an extensive rebuttal to these, and a simple "it is beyond the scope of this essay to address this objection," and the addition of a footnote referencing those who make such an objection, will often suffice. Good essays end by providing a summary of the essay's thesis and main points, as well as recommending new questions for further research, as appropriate. There is no cut and dry answer to the question of how many academic sources are required since this will depend upon how sources are used and the scope of the argument.

Tarak's Tree

The aforementioned Tarak Barkawi introduced me to a wonderful mnemonic for helping less experienced student researchers think about the necessary elements of a research paper. Since it takes the form of a Christmas tree, I call this mnemonic "Tarak's Tree" in honor of him.

The base of the tree is the research question. Connected perpendicularly to the base is the trunk of the tree, which represents the thesis or answer to the research question.

Along the sides of the trunk, supporting the thesis, are branches which represent the argument's main points. Along each branch are ornaments that represent the data used to support each main point, whether that data is newly gathered or referenced from another academic's work. At the top of the tree is the star which represents the self-critical standpoint that is required of any academic essay. That is, the star represents the need to make any assumptions explicit and to be humble by being up front about both the strengths and the weaknesses of one's findings.

Despite its simplicity, many new researchers forget one or another element of Tarak's Tree. In so doing, they fail to convey information that is essential to their research project. Writing in accordance with this image needn't be mechanical and spiritless. However, inexperienced researchers are advised to wait until the inclusion of these elements becomes ingrained and habitual before they begin introducing literary flair and stylistic panache to their writing.

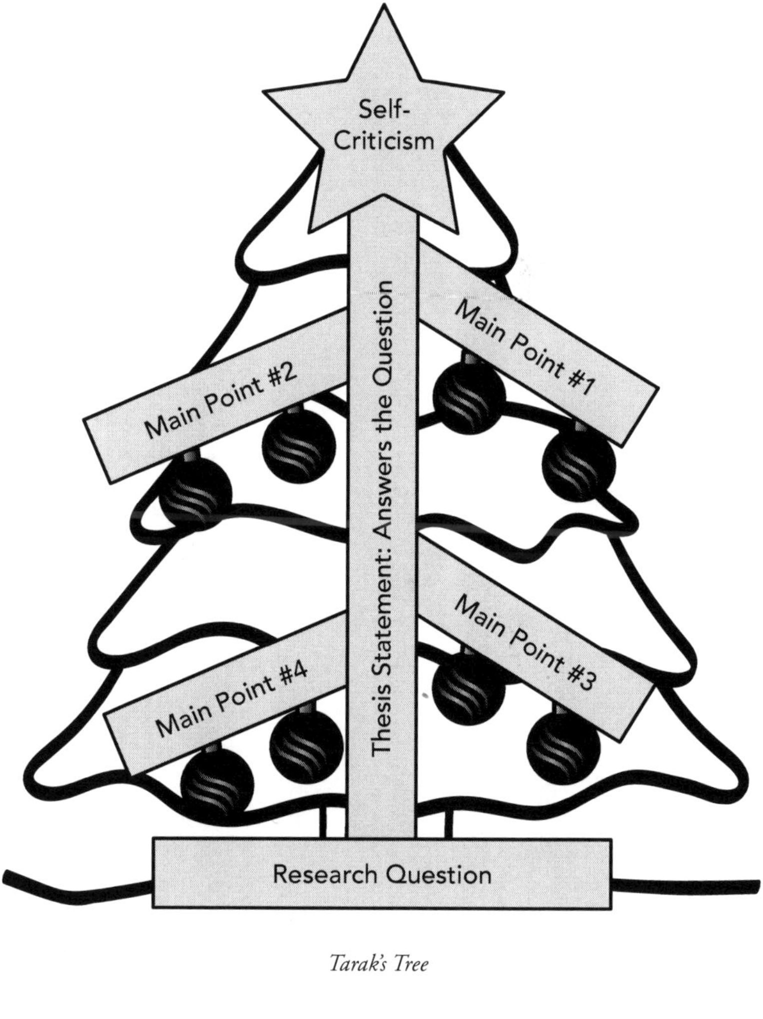
Self-
Criticism
Thesis Statement: Answers the Question
Main Point #1
Main Point #2
Main Point #3
Main Point #4
Research Question

Tarak's Tree

CONCLUSION

Each of the seven steps discussed in this book is the subject of entire treatises that invariably provide detailed and thoughtful discussions of the techniques utilized and pitfalls encountered at each step. For example, there are books of several hundred pages in length that map out a six step process (sometimes more) simply for conducting a literature review. There are also hundred page books advising students on the most optimal methods for constructing research questions. Reference guides and style manuals, such as *The Elements of Style* by William Strunk Jr. and E.B. White (2003), sit comfortably on bookshelves next to subject-specific guides to writing. All of these are helpful additions to a researcher's reference library.

This book, by contrast, sought to inform readers about the essential information necessary to conduct successful research. Specifically, it focused on elucidating the very process of research: its seven steps. The goal has been to provide readers with a macro-level overview—a guiding map—that empowers their research project by showing them, straightforwardly, the contours of the road. Since each step along that road depends upon its predecessor, glimpsing the whole best prepares researchers to begin their journey.

BIBLIOGRAPHY

Ayer, A. J. 1959. "Verification and Experience." In *Logical Positivism*, edited by A.J. Ayer, 1959. New York: The Free Press, pp.228-243.

Bridgman, Percy Williams. 1927. *The Logic of Modern Physics*. New York: MacMillan.

Buckley, William F. 1986. "I Am Lapidary But Not Eristic When I Use Big Words," *New York Times,* 30 Nov. 1986. Accessed 10 April 2020: http://movies2.nytimes.com/books/00/07/16/specials/buckley-bigwords.html

Emerson, Ralph Waldo. 2000. "Character." In *The Essential Writings of Ralph Waldo Emerson*. New York: Random House, pp. 528-535.

Feyerabend, Paul. 2010. *Against Method (Fourth Edition).* New York: Verso Books.

Gustafson, K. C. 2010. "Echo of Empires: Russia's Inheritance of Byzantine Security Culture." *Journal of Slavic Military Studies* 23(4): 574-596.

Hatfield, Joseph. 2017. "An Ethical Defense of Treason by Means of Espionage." *Intelligence and National Security* 32 (2): 195-207.

Jackson, Patrick Thaddeus. 2016. *The Conduct of Inquiry in International Relations (Second Edition)*, New York: Routledge.

Lewis, C. S. 2001. "The Inner Ring." In *The Weight of Glory: And Other Addresses*. New York: Harper Collins, pp. 141-157.

King, Gary, Robert O. Keohane, and Sydney Verba. 1994. *Designing Social Inquiry: Scientific Inference in Qualitative Research*. Princeton, NJ: Princeton University Press.

Kuhn, Thomas S. 1996. *The Structure of Scientific Revolutions (Third Edition)*. Chicago: University of Chicago Press.

Mueller, Pam A., and Daniel M. Oppenheimer. 2014. "The Pen is Mightier than the Keyboard: Advantages of Longhand over Laptop Note Taking." *Psychological Science* 25(6): 1-10.

Orwell, George. 1981. "Politics and the English Language." New York: Houghton Mifflin Harcourt, pp. 156-170.

Poe, Edgar Allan. 1846. "The Philosophy of Composition." *Graham's Magazine*, vol. 28, no. 4, April 1846: 163-167. Accessed 10 April 2020: https://www.eapoe.org/works/essays/philcomp.htm.

Neurath, Otto. 1959. "Protocol Sentences." In *Logical Positivism*, edited by A.J. Ayer, 1959. New York: The Free Press, pp. 199-208.

Quine, W.V.O., and J. S. Ullian. 1978. *The Web of Belief* (Second Edition). New York: McGraw-Hill, particularly pp. 20-49.

Rachels, James. 2019. "The Challenge of Cultural Relativism." In *The Elements of Moral Philosophy* (Ninth Edition), New York: McGraw-Hill., pp. 14-31.

Rorty, Richard. 1982. "Philosophy as a Kind of Writing: an essay on Derrida." In *Consequences of Pragmatism*. Minneapolis: University of Minnesota Press, pp. 90-109.

Sellars, Wilfrid. 1956. *Empiricism and the Philosophy of Mind*. Minneapolis: University of Minnesota Press.

Strunk, Jr., William, and E.B. White. 2003. *The Elements of Style (Fourth Edition)*. London: Pearson.

John R. Trimble. 2010. *Writing with Style: Conversations on the Art of Writing (3rd Edition)*. New York: Pearson.

Welch, Stephen. 2013. "Political Culture." In *Intelligence Elsewhere: Spies and Espionage outside the Anglosphere*, Philip H. J. Davies and Kristian C. Gustafson (Editors), pp. 13-26.

Walzer, Michael. 1973. "Political Action: The Problem of Dirty Hands." *Philosophy & Public Affairs*, Vol. 2, No. 2, pp. 160-180.

Wheeler, Donald J. 2000. *Understanding Variation* (Second Edition). Knoxville, TN: SPC Press.

ABOUT THE AUTHOR

Joseph M. Hatfield (Ph.D. University of Cambridge) is the Associate Chair of the Department of Cyber Science at the U.S. Naval Academy, where he teaches courses on the technical foundations of cyber-security, human factors in cyber operations, and intelligence and national security. As an active-duty naval intelligence officer with more than a decade of overseas operational experience, his intelligence research has informed senior governmental decision makers, including analysis sent directly to the President of the United States. His research is published widely in peer-reviewed academic journals. He is also a recipient of the Rear Admiral Thomas A. Brooks Intelligence Officer of the Year Award and the Alfred Thayer Mahan Award for Literary Achievement.